A souvenir guide

The White Cliffs of Dover and South Foreland Lighthouse

Kent

National Trust

A national treasure

'Whoever visits this place cannot fail to receive a still further pleasure, from the views of the high and stupendous white cliffs along the shore, and the grandeur of the neighbouring hills, of the azure sea, with the moving prospect on it, bounded by the variegated Boulogne hills, on the coast of France; and from the continued novelty afforded, in the time of peace, by the packets and passage-boats to and from France, almost every hour, filled with passengers of every rank and country.'

Edward Hasted, historian of Kent, 1800

One of England's most cherished landmarks, the White Cliffs of Dover have long occupied a special place in the nation's cultural identity. Towering above the English Channel with far-ranging views across to France, this stretch of stunning chalk-buttressed coastline has come to symbolise British pride and determination to defend its coast against all comers.

Today, the cliffs are treasured no less as a place of immense natural beauty. Here flower-studded cliff-top grasslands meet an ever-changing seascape beneath a theatre of clouds and sunlight.

A watery beginning
The origin of the White Cliffs

The story of the chalk cliffs begins some 65–80 million years ago, when an ocean covered much of present-day Europe. The warm tropical climate that prevailed at this time provided ideal conditions for a rich oceanic 'soup' of microscopic organisms to thrive. Many of these were composed of calcium carbonate. Over millions of years the accumulation of these fossilised organisms on the sea bed solidified to form the thick deposits of the soft white limestone we now know as chalk.

Over an immense period of time, what is now south-east England was subject to

geological forces which pushed up the region to form an elongated dome running roughly west to east. This dome encompassed the North and South Downs, the fringes of the Butser Hills in Hampshire to the west and, to the east, the Bas-Boullanais region of northern France. At the mercy of rain, snow and ice, this 'tableland' of chalk was gradually eroded to leave the ranges of the North and South Downs that we see today.

Left Langdon Cliffs
Opposite The White Cliffs at dawn
Below The formation of the White Cliffs

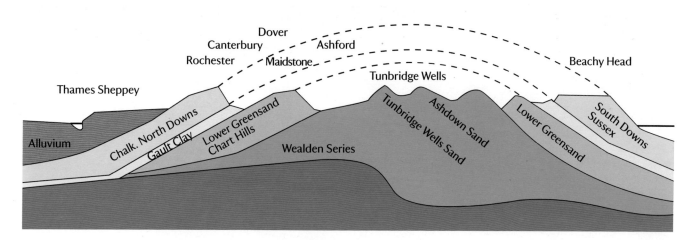

A world of chalk

'Sat 16 Feb 1799 This week there was a very great fall of the cliff exact between the soldiers and the officers subterraneous barracks where the opening is between to give light to the Well it fell down quite from the top of the Cliff a very great way. This day in the forenoon it was discovered that unknown to any person in the night, a bank of chalk and earth had fell down by the frost and thaw and filled one of the huts in the Castle, whereby an Artillery man and his wife were suffocated as they lay in bed, the infant child was preserved and taken out alive.'

From Thomas Pattenden's diary

An island is born

Standing only 21 miles distant and visible on a clear day, the cliffs of Cap Gris-Nez and Blanc-Nez bear testament to the former land-bridge that once connected Britain with mainland Europe. When and how the breach of the sea occurred is a matter of much speculation. One theory is that it resulted from a catastrophic flood during one of the glaciations of the Ice Age, about half a million years ago. A huge ice sheet had spread across northern Britain and the North Sea, damming a vast lake against the chalk hills. The lake filled until it overtopped the lowest point, gouging a deep channel through the hills. As the ice sheet melted, the sea gradually spread back up the English Channel. Eventually, the rising seawater flooded the lake overflow channel, which became the Strait of Dover.

Cliffs in retreat

Exposed to the wear and tear of the elements and battered by storm waves, year by year the cliff line is slowly retreating. By and large this retreat is barely noticeable but occasionally great chunks can be lost in a sudden cliff fall, sometimes with disastrous consequences.

character of the rock. In the later 19th century geologists developed this further and eventually found a more accurate way of classifying different layers by using fossils found within the chalk to identify different zones. The 'Lower', 'Middle' and 'Upper' divisions of chalk are the terms that are used today.

Flints are a characteristic rock found in seams within the chalk cliff-faces at Dover. They are believed to have been formed from the remains of silica-based creatures such as sea sponges. Most of the beach pebbles at the foot of the cliffs today are flints, smoothed and rounded by the pounding of the waves. Look out for flints in the local architecture around Dover. They can be seen in churches, walls and houses throughout the area.

Above Knapped flint is a popular local building material

Right The geologist William Phillips pioneered our understanding of how chalk was formed

Opposite Blocks of chalk regularly fall from the cliffs, restoring their whiteness

'These cliffs afford one of the best opportunities for studying the chalk formation which can anywhere be found.'

William Phillips, 1822

A geologist's paradise

Ever since the days of early 19th-century interest in geology, the White Cliffs of Dover have offered one of the most accessible and complete records of the story of chalk formation. Early geologists realised that different conditions at the time of the formation of the chalk produced different types of chalk layers. William Phillips's description of the cliffs between Folkestone and Walmer in 1822 was one of the earliest attempts to divide English chalk into these layers. He distinguished different bands, based on a crude description of the

Nature's treasure chest

Blackcap

Whitethroat

The cliff-top grasslands have long been cherished for their breathtaking splendour in spring and summer, when wildflowers of every hue jostle for space amongst the thyme-scented turf. Clouds of butterflies and the hypnotic high-summer chorus of buzzing bees and chirruping grasshoppers make the cliff-top experience a true feast for the senses.

The rich natural heritage owes much to the special characteristics of the chalk-loving plants that thrive in the dry and poor growing conditions here. Wildflowers such as salad burnet and horseshoe vetch have extensive root systems that help them to tap into sources of moisture deep within the soil. Others such as eyebright and rockrose grow close to the ground to take advantage of the more humid atmosphere near the soil. Amongst the less common plants here are the nationally rare early spider orchid, meadow clary and oxtongue broomrape.

Such a wealth of wildflowers naturally attracts an abundance of insect life, none more treasured than the many butterflies and moths. The cliffs here are home to around 30 different species of butterfly. Like miniature gems amongst the downland turf, the tribe of the 'blue' butterflies – adonis, chalkhill, common and small – is a particular treat to spot in the summer months.

Did you know?
Such is the diversity of wildflowers that one square metre of chalk grassland can support as many as 40 different plants. This is more than in a tropical rainforest.

Kittiwake

Linnet

Raven

Skylark

Chalkhill blue butterfly

Adonis blue butterfly

Early spider orchid

Juniper

A home for the summer

The patchwork of grasslands and thickets is the favoured haunt for a rich variety of bird-life. Skylark, meadow pippit, linnet and yellowhammer are joined in spring by blackcap, whitethroat and other warblers. The cliff-top grasslands and thickets provide a welcome landfall for many of these migrants, exhausted after their long journeys. Some stay and breed.

Cliff-side life

Just as the grasslands are home to many plants and animals, so too are the precipitous cliff-sides. The salt-laden winds that whip up from the shoreline make for a fascinating array of salt-tolerant plants such as wild cabbage and hoary stock, which cling to the nooks and crannies of the cliff. These ledges also provide safe roosting and nesting sites for seabirds such as lesser black-backed gulls, fulmars and over 1,100 pairs of kittiwakes. Look out too for that most fearsome of aerial hunters, the peregrine falcon, which is now a regular resident on the cliffs around Dover. In times past, both chough and raven also nested on the rocky and turf-clad ledges of the cliffs.

Living on the edge

The cliffs nearby are home to one of the rarest plants in the county. Juniper is a coniferous shrub native to the British Isles, which grows on bare limestone soils. Once a widespread shrub on the North Downs of Kent, it is now restricted to a hundred or so plants found in just two localities. One of these occurs near Langdon Cliffs. The National Trust carefully manages the area to encourage young juniper seedlings to become established.

Return of the raven

The raven is a member of the crow family with a large bill and a wingspan of up to 130cm (about the same size as a buzzard). Once a regular breeding bird in Kent, it gradually disappeared through persecution and habitat loss in the second half of the 19th century. For decades it has remained confined to the mountains and moorlands of western and northern England. Yet, remarkably, for the first time in 120 years, ravens returned in 2009 to breed on the cliffs at Dover.

The White Cliffs in war and peace

Invaders and immigrants

Ever since the earliest settlers plied to and forth across the Strait of Dover, the cliffs have kept a watchful eye on man's comings and goings.

Landings ...

The earliest written record of the White Cliffs appears in 55BC, when Julius Caesar made his first expedition to Britain across the Channel and encountered the 'armed forces of the enemy displayed on all the cliffs'. It was the threat of being hit by missiles that could be hurled from the overlooking cliffs that discouraged Caesar from landing at Dover. He eventually found better moorings in the open waters around the low-lying coast near Deal.

Having conquered Britain, the Romans soon established Dover as a port and military base. This set in train a long and colourful chapter in the history of the port as a strategic and vital link with continental Europe. The cliffs witnessed a steady stream of monarchs, merchants and noblemen throughout the Norman, medieval and Tudor periods. Some passed through to visit their French territories. Some left to embark on perilous crusades, while others arrived upon these shores to claim the English throne.

Over the centuries many refugees and immigrants have landed at Dover, and the White Cliffs were their first glimpse of a new home and future. In 1685 thousands of Huguenots (French Protestants) landed at Dover to escape persecution in Europe.

An unwelcome visitor

During the late Middle Ages the town played host to another, not so welcome visitor in the form of the Black Death. Ports such as Dover, where ships, merchants and seamen crossed paths from all corners of the continent, bore the brunt of plague epidemics and suffered many casualties. Local legend records that during the outbreak in the mid-1660s, when the plague was at its peak, soldiers at the nearby Archcliffe fort on the opposite side of the harbour were so fearful that they rang bells, fired guns and lit fires to try and scare the plague away.

Below left Captain Matthew Webb was the first person to swim the Channel, in 1875

Below right The French balloonist Jean-Pierre Blanchard made the first aerial crossing of the Channel, in 1785

Left Henry VIII embarked at Dover to meet the French king Francis I at the Field of Cloth of Gold in 1520

Below Julius Caesar was the first writer to describe the White Cliffs

... and crossings

For a neck of sea only 21 miles across at its narrowest, the Channel has presented a surprisingly stiff challenge to all who have tried to cross its treacherous waters in anything other than a boat. As the most primitive means of crossing, it was not until 1875 that the first ever cross-channel swim was completed. Backed by three chase boats and smeared in porpoise oil, Captain Matthew Webb battled through strong currents, freezing temperatures and jellyfish shoals, eventually completing his crossing in a time of 21 hours and 45 minutes.

The first aerial crossing was made by the French balloonist Jean-Pierre Blanchard from Dover to Calais in 1785. Over one hundred years later on an early summer's morning in 1909, Louis Blériot touched down in a field next to the castle, marking the first heavier-than-air-flight crossing. This heralded the beginning of a new era in air, sea and human powered crossings of all forms – conventional and eccentric.

A 'fixed' land link in the form of a subterranean tunnel between England and France had occupied many people's minds during the 19th and 20th centuries. After numerous failed attempts, the construction of the first underground crossing – the Channel Tunnel – was finally accomplished on 6 May 1994.

Timeline
1216 Siege of Dover Castle by Louis, Dauphin of France
1415 Henry V landed at Dover after Agincourt
1460 Earl of Warwick landed at Dover to lead Yorkist army
1520 Henry VIII left Dover for the Field of Cloth of Gold
1621 First Huguenot refugees arrived
1660 Charles II landed at Dover for the Restoration
1815 Duke of Wellington landed at Dover after Waterloo

Did you know?
The name 'English Channel' has been widely used since the early 18th century, possibly originating from the designation *Engelse Kanaal* on Dutch sea maps.

Inmates and industry (1884–96)

The mid-19th century marked the onset of a period of great transformation on the cliff-top. This was a time when grand plans were afoot for the expansion of the harbour at Dover. It was also a time when convict labour was in plentiful supply. The White Cliffs offered tempting possibilities …

Paying debts to society

After Dover had been earmarked as the site for a new harbour for the Navy, it made perfect sense to use the ever-growing prison labour force to build it. Transportation to the colonies had come to an end, and new prison sites were being sought. An ideal opportunity arose when the Ecclesiastical Commissioners sold a plot of the cliff-top land in 1883 to the government, and work began straightaway on building a new prison here. By September 1885 the first convicts had arrived, but they were never employed in the building of the harbour. The grand plans for the new harbour soon ground to a halt because of lack of government support. Most of the convicts were employed on more menial tasks such as sewing mailbags, making bedding and chopping firewood. The prison's days were inevitably numbered: within ten years it had closed, and the last inmates had been moved to other sites around the country.

'Hard bed, hard board, hard labour'

The 19th century saw a radical reform of the punishment system in England. When transportation ended in the 1830s, many prisoners were kept in disused warships known as 'hulks', but overcrowding meant that a new prison-building programme was needed. Between 1840 and 1877 around 90 prisons were built, at great public expense. Many new ideas were tried in answer to the old problem of what to do with those who break the law. These included solitary confinement, and in the latter part of the 19th century, 'hard bed, hard board and hard labour', in which inmates endured hard plank beds, and were forced to undertake monotonous tasks.

The four terraces around the Visitor Centre mark the ranges of the prison buildings. Cells occupied the first and third levels. The second terrace comprised the laundry, bake-house and bath-house at one end and an exercise area. The foundations of further buildings survive amongst the scrub and garden areas including apple trees and strawberry plants.

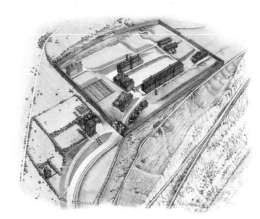

Above Bird's-eye-view reconstruction of the prison by the cliffs

Left Langdon Prison

Soldiers behind bars (1901–9)

Broadleas Military Prison

The closure of the prison in 1896 was met with much concern. Feelings ran high in Parliament as the site and buildings had cost almost £45,000, and now were seemingly no longer needed. It was decided to hand the site over to the Army, which re-opened it as Broadleas Military Prison in 1901.

Its new inmates were offenders of a different kind. A grim and foreboding prospect for any serviceman, Broadleas became a well-known detention barracks for dishonoured and court-martialled soldiers from all ranks and regiments.

Further additions were made at this time, including an enlarged house for the governor, a stable block, gymnasium, drill hall, warder's house and workshops. The foundations of these buildings can still be seen today. Its new-found purpose, however, was short-lived, for by 1909 it had closed, and the corridors, drill squares and workshops no longer echoed to the sound of barked orders and time-served labour, but once again returned to the peace of cliff-top breeze and larksong.

Keeping order

Responsibility for the running of the prison lay with the prison governor and his right-hand man, the chief warder. The governor and his family lived just outside the prison wall in an impressive three-storey, double-fronted house called Mount Kemmel. Such a high-status job afforded privileges and luxuries far beyond those of the prison staff. The house boasted its own tennis courts and a croquet lawn. The outline of these can still just be seen.

> **Did you know?**
> Military prisons were first established in 1844 'to avoid the necessity of mixing soldiers sentenced for military offences with the ordinary criminals in county gaols'.

Above The governor's family

Left Originally used as a workshop, after the prison closed, the building housed a large engine that powered the lights on the eastern side of the docks

The Red House

The chief warder and his assistants were responsible for the day-to-day overseeing of the inmates. He lived just outside the confines of the prison wall and had a small, comfortable house typical of the Edwardian period. The footprint of the rooms and the remains of the red quarry tiles at the doorway can still be seen.

Left The Red House was built for the chief warder of the military prison

Below The staff of the military prison

From barracks to battery (1914–45)

A new chapter in the cliff's history gradually unfolded during the early 20th century. This heralded a period of unprecedented cliff-top activity, when the peacetime sounds of industry and labour were replaced by the sights and sounds of a nation at war.

Langdon Barracks (1914–18)

The onset of the First World War witnessed a new lease of life for the derelict prison buildings. The site was brought back into use as a transit camp for soldiers on their way to the Western Front in Flanders. It soon became clear, however, that the old and cramped prison cells were far from ideal accommodation, and the lack of space meant that many soldiers spent their last days in England living in tents. By 1924 it was decided to demolish most of the buildings and rebuild a new barracks just below the castle, leaving just Mount Kemmel, the infirmary, sheds and storehouses standing.

Langdon Battery

By the Second World War these buildings were used as headquarters and sergeants' mess for the nearby anti-aircraft battery. This was located close to the present-day coastguard station.

The battery was armed with two or three six-inch guns, all carefully positioned to cover an extensive arc of fire over the Channel waters. Furnished with three searchlight positions and an observation post set into the cliffs, it soon became one of the most formidable gun batteries protecting the harbour. A honeycomb of tunnels connected the battery, observation post and other emplacements with the eastern docks and the castle.

Railway guns

A wartime use was soon found for the cliff-top railway line that had once served the harbour building projects. With its days of transporting ballast and sand all but a distant memory, its new-found role saw it carrying a cargo of a much more deadly kind. This was in the form of five large railway-served guns. They included 'Winnie' (which fired the first shell from England to France) and 'Pooh'.

Above Langdon Barracks

Below During the Second World War, the entire south-east coast of England became a fortress with gun emplacements such as these

Opposite 'Winnie', one of the railway-served guns, in action

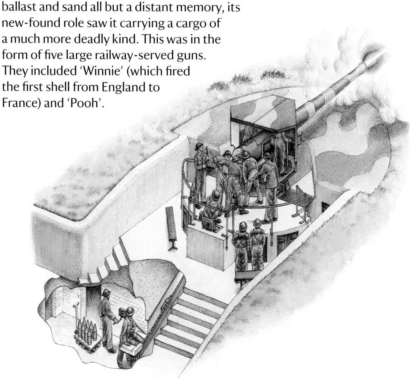

Hellfire Corner' (1939–45)

Today's uncluttered cliff-top views and peaceful grasslands are a far cry from the hustle and bustle that would have surrounded this area in the Second World War. Imagine a time when pillboxes, trenches, observation posts, and tunnels would have filled the view, all laced with the ensnaring cobwebs of barbed wire.

This front-line position set the scene for one of the most sustained onslaughts of enemy firepower during the Second World War. For this was a time when Dover and its neighbourhood fell victim to bombardment from air, land and sea – a fate immortalised in its unenviable nickname of 'Hellfire Corner'. The White Cliffs gained a new meaning for returning fighter pilots, bomber crews, soldiers and sailors as 'home' and a place of safety.

Of all these homeward crossings, none was more symbolic than the evacuation of Dunkirk in May 1940. The cliffs formed the welcoming backdrop to over 200,000 troops, who were dramatically rescued from the beaches, just hours before the town of Dunkirk fell into enemy hands.

Opposite left Second World War telephone exchange in one of the tunnels beneath Dover Castle

Opposite right Winston Churchill inspecting the Dover defences in August 1940. An air raid was in progress at the time

Below Exhausted troops arriving back in Dover harbour after being rescued from Dunkirk in May 1940

A subterranean world

For centuries the assortment of defences above the cliff-top has been quietly, and often secretly, accompanied by a slowly growing labyrinth of caves, passages and tunnels beneath. Medieval defenders of the cliff-top and castle were quick to recognise the easy workability of the soft chalk rock. Tunnels were excavated to give protected passage and concealment for defending armies and provide that most coveted tactic of warfare – the element of surprise.

By the time of the outbreak of the Second World War, the tunnels had echoed to a multitude of occupants and uses. They had resounded with the footfall of resident Napoleonic soldiers; they had witnessed skirmishes and gun fights between smugglers and the authorities' coastal blockade men; and they had provided storage and shelter for the First World War Fire Command Post and gun batteries. But it was the Second World War that saw their ultimate potential fulfilled, when their secure and well-protected caverns provided the ideal headquarters for coastal and anti-aircraft operation centres. It was from these headquarters that Vice-Admiral Ramsay coordinated the evacuation plan for Dunkirk known as 'Operation Dynamo'.

Innovation and excavation (1900–25)

Treasured today for their peace and tranquillity, the cliffs were once the scene of industry and innovation of earth-moving proportions.

Right Richard Tilden Smith, who devised the aerial ropeway

Below Artist's impression of the aerial ropeway

The 'aerial ropeway'

Arguably one of the most ambitious and innovative schemes that the cliffs have played host to was the 'aerial ropeway'. This was an astounding feat of engineering that allowed coal to be transported from the east Kent coalfields to the harbour. The planning, design and construction of this impressive structure was all down to the dreams and determination of the industrialist Richard Tilden Smith. He realised that the only way to turn round the ailing fortunes of the collieries at Tilmanstone was to find a way of transporting coal to the dockside that avoided the crippling freight charges of the railway line. Tilden Smith's plans were to create a seven-and-a-half-mile 'ropeway' over farmland, cutting two tunnels down through the cliffs to take the coal straight to the dock. The first buckets were loaded with coal in February 1930, but sadly Tilden Smith never lived to see his dreams fulfilled, dying just months before its completion. Although the ropeway was well equipped for the task, the exports of coal failed to meet expectations, and the grand project fell into disuse. By the end of the war the derelict structure was beyond repair and it was eventually broken up in 1954 and sold for scrap.

Above The cliff-side railway

Making tracks
The building of the harbour

Wide grassy terraces cut into the chalk face of the cliff are all that remain of a time in the early 1900s when the area was the backdrop to a huge construction project. Picture a scene of men and machines excavating chalk from the cliff-face and steam locomotives puffing their way up the cliff-side. For this was a time of great change around the harbour, when projects such as the Admiralty Pier construction required the delivery of vast quantities of ballast, shingle and chalk. In 1898–9 S. Pearson & Son built a track from the main railway line at Martin Mill across the cliff-top land. This allowed ballast and shingle to be transported to cliffs above the docks from far afield, along with chalk, which was dug straight from the sheer faces of the towering cliffs.

The line was dismantled in 1937 after the harbour was completed but was then relaid again in the Second World War to provide firing positions for track-mounted guns.

Did you know?
The aerial ropeway was capable of moving 120 tons of coal per hour; buckets were spaced 46 yards apart and left the colliery every 21 seconds.

South Foreland Lighthouse

A familiar landmark for miles around, South Foreland Lighthouse is testimony to the centuries-old tradition of guiding ships safely through the treacherous waters of the Dover Strait.

A cliff-top beacon

The first cliff-top beacons date as far back as the Roman period, when two 'lighthouses' were constructed at Dover to guide Roman seafarers safely into port. Remains of one can still be seen next to the church of St Mary-in-Castro within the grounds of Dover Castle. Later periods saw the use of simple cliff-top beacon fires, one of which was maintained in the 14th century by a hermit who lived in a cave in the nearby village of St Margaret's Bay. The first record of a permanent structure on the current-day lighthouse site is around 1635, when two wooden towers were erected to support an iron basket and coal fire. Modifications over the next 150 years incorporated brick, flint, glazing and, in 1793, the use of oil lamps. In the 1840s, under the ownership of Trinity House, the corporation that maintains all the lighthouses in England

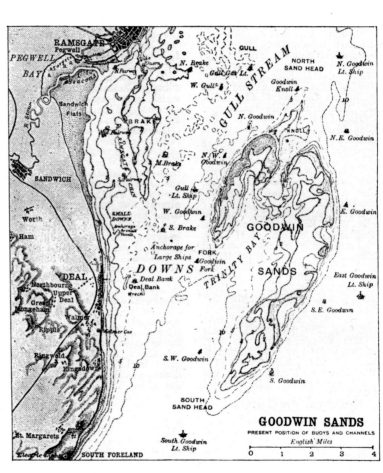

Above Goodwin Sands *c.*1900

Left The Great Storm of 1703

Opposite South Foreland Lighthouse

and Wales, the structure was rebuilt in Portland stone. This new lighthouse worked in conjunction with a second lighthouse, situated nearer the cliff edge, to guide ships safely around the Goodwin Sands.

'The shippe swallower'

Since prehistoric seafarers first plied their way to and forth across this narrow neck of sea, its ever-shifting sand-banks and treacherous rock-littered foreshores have claimed many lives. The most notorious area is the Goodwin Sands, once known as 'the shippe swallower', a ten-mile-long sand-bank situated just three miles off the coast. Some of its banks lie so close to the surface that hapless vessels have been known to be engulfed and sucked down into the sands within a day. Within these shoals lie the wrecks of over 2,000 ships, 50 of which were claimed in the Great Storm of 1703. This was one of the worst storms to hit southern England in recorded history and is said to have claimed the lives of over 2,000 sailors on the Sands.

Just a stone's throw from Langdon Cliffs lies the site of one of the earliest ship-wrecks known in Britain. Imagine a scene over 3,000 years ago when a Bronze Age trader, caught in the surge and swell of a heavy sea, lost his vessel to the waves, which littered the seabed with over 350 bronze tools and weapons. This wreck remained undiscovered until recent times. Testament to the unforgiving nature of the sea are the visible remains of more recent victims. Just below South Foreland can be seen the battered relic of the five-masted SS *Preussen* wrecked in 1910. Closer to the cliff at Langdon Bay lies the shattered hulk of the SS *Falcon*, a steamer which caught fire in 1926.

Did you know?
According to local legend, the schooner *Lady Lovibond* was wrecked on the Goodwin Sands in 1748 with all hands lost. She is said to reappear every 50 years as a ghost ship.

A room with a view

Although only 69 feet high, South Foreland Lighthouse boasted the title of the highest light in England and Wales simply because it stands on a 300-foot-high cliff. It comprises the generator room (originally used to store oil for the light), weights room, watch room and lamp room. The oil stored in the generator room originally came from sperm whales. When this became more expensive in the mid-19th century, an alternative in the form of rapeseed oil was used. A pioneer of its time, the lighthouse was also the first to use an electric light. This ground-breaking advance owes much to the inspiration of Michael Faraday, who was Scientific Adviser to Trinity House. A separate engine house with steam-powered generators built in 1872 provided electricity until the advent of mains electricity in 1922. This marked another claim to fame for the lighthouse as the first in the country to be powered by that means. It was also the first to use incandescent lamps.

Did you know?
The alternating pattern of blackout panels and lenses gives each lighthouse its own individual signal so that ships can easily identify their position.

Above South Foreland Lighthouse in action

Right The drive mechanism for the lantern

Let there be light

Before the days of electricity and lenses, light was focused out to sea by the simple means of a reflector on the landward side of the oil lamp. When the lighthouse was converted from a fixed light to a flashing light, an ingenious arrangement of weights and cables was installed to provide the power to rotate the lenses (known as the optic). Using a winding handle mounted in the lamp room, the keeper raised a 1/4 ton weight to the top of a central column. Then, through the simple action of gravity, the weight gradually descended, so powering the rotation of the platform on which the lenses stood. As these moved around the lamp, a flashing effect was produced.

Vigilance was called for at all times, as the weight took only two and a half hours to descend, before which point it needed to be rewound to the top. An electric winder was eventually fitted in the 1920s, and the lighthouse was fully automated in 1969.

The Marconi connection

Of all its pioneering 'firsts', South Foreland Lighthouse's special claim to fame lies in a Christmas greeting transmitted on 24 December 1898. For this simple exchange of festive tidings was in the form of the first-ever two-way ship-to-shore radio message using Morse code. The brains behind this achievement was the celebrated inventor Guglielmo Marconi, who foresaw the tremendous potential of wireless telegraphy for sending signals offshore. The importance of this ground-breaking achievement, made first between the East Goodwin lightship and South Foreland Lighthouse, was fully realised the following year. Then, for the first time in history, lifeboats at Ramsgate and Deal were alerted to a ship in distress by the medium of telegraph. The same year witnessed the first international wireless transmission, sent from Wimereux in France and received at South Foreland Lighthouse.

End of an era

Three keepers originally manned the lighthouse and each worked a two-day shift. Their jobs included keeping the lamp lit and optic turning, as well as cleaning, polishing and keeping the logbooks up-to-date. Most of the keepers' time was spent in the watch room. Little by little the keepers' jobs were replaced by new technology and automation. South Foreland Lighthouse continued to operate until 1988, when the ever-growing sophistication of computers and satellite navigation systems eventually made it redundant.

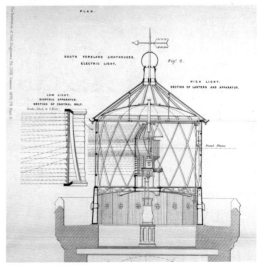

Top Guglielmo Marconi in the 1890s

Above The South Foreland Lighthouse lamp

Caring for the cliffs

Below Exmoor ponies
grazing the grasslands

Bottom Wildflowers
flourish by a coastal path
above the White Cliffs

Chewing the cud

The flower-rich grasslands of the cliffs owe their very existence to the age-old tradition of livestock grazing. For it is only through the regular browsing of sheep, cattle and horses that the ever-encroaching thickets of bushes and trees are kept at bay and that the fine chalk grassland flowers are able to thrive. Managing the grazing calls for a careful balance: too little and the coarse grasses, bushes and trees take hold; too much and the delicate plants are unable to flower and set seed. In times past these cliff-top grasslands would have formed extensive pastures for sheep. Today they are maintained through the National Trust's own herd of Exmoor ponies. This hardy breed is particularly good at keeping in check the coarse grasses and shrubs.

People power

The White Cliffs of Dover and South Foreland Lighthouse are privileged to receive committed and ongoing support from a large number of dedicated volunteers. Their unstinting efforts enable the chalk grassland to be actively managed to balance conservation and access, and the site as a whole to offer an exciting range of experiences for visitors to this extraordinary place. There are over 55,000 National Trust volunteers in England, Wales and Northern Ireland. If you are interested in learning more about the benefits of volunteering at your local property, please contact the White Cliffs office on 01304 207326 or South Foreland Lighthouse on 01304 852463.